# FIERCE DINOSAURS!

## The Theropods

WORLD
BOOK

A Scott Fetzer company

Chicago

**www.worldbook.com**

For information about other World Book publications,
visit our website at http://www.worldbookonline.com
or call **1-800-WORLDBK (967-5325)**.

For information about sales to schools and libraries,
call **1-800-975-3250** (United States), or **1-800-837-5365** (Canada).

© 2013, 2006 Amber Books Ltd., London

World Book, Inc.
233 N. Michigan Ave.
Chicago, IL 60601

Amber Books Ltd.
74-77 White Lion Street
London N1 9PF
United Kingdom
www.amberbooks.co.uk

Library of Congress Cataloging-in-Publication Data

Fierce dinosaurs : the large Theropods.
     p. cm. -- (Dinosaurs!)
   Summary: "An introduction to large theropods, a group of dinosaurs
that walked on two legs and that included the meat-eating dinosaurs.
Features include an original drawing of each dinosaur, fun facts, a
glossary, and a list of additional resources"-- Provided by publisher.
   Includes index.
   ISBN 978-0-7166-0369-6
   1. Saurischia--Juvenile literature. 2. Carnivorous animals, Fossil--
Juvenile literature. 3. Paleontology--Jurassic--Juvenile literature.
4. Paleontology--Cretaceous--Juvenile literature.  I. World Book, Inc.
   QE862.S3F537 2013
   567.912--dc23
                    2012016115
Dinosaurs
Set ISBN  978-0-7166-0366-5
Printed in China by Toppan Leefung Printing Ltd.,
Guangdong Province
1st printing September 2012

# Contents

The long, sharp claw of Baryonyx *(above)* demonstrates the great size and fearsome nature of large theropods. The massive skull of the theropod Carchardontosaurus dwarfs paleontologist Paul Sereno, whose team found the fossil in the Moroccan Sahara *(opposite)*.

# Introduction

About 150 million years ago, on the plains of what is now western North America, one of the most fearsome *predators* (meat-eaters) of all time hides among the trees, watching a young Stegosaurus eat ferns. Mighty Allosaurus reaches more than 30 feet (9 meters) long, and weighs more than 2 tons (1.8 metric tons). The fierce predator readies its dangerous claws, some of which reach about 10 inches (25 centimeters) long. Suddenly, Allosaurus lunges forward to attack. The young Stegosaurus tries to fight back, thrashing about with its spiked tail. But this Allosaurus is an experienced hunter. It delivers a devastating strike to the neck, toppling its victim. After a few twitches, the Stegosaurus falls still, and the Allosaurus begins to feast.

Allosaurus was a type of dinosaur called a theropod *(THAIR-uh-pod)*. All meat-eating dinosaurs were theropods. Most were powerfully built. Theropods walked upright on their two hind legs, and many kinds could run quickly. Their relatively short arms ended in hands that could grasp objects. Nearly all theropods had a long, muscular tail, which they used for balance. However, theropods varied greatly in size. The smallest theropods were only about the size of a chicken. The largest theropods were far longer and heavier than any predator alive today. Such giant dinosaurs as Allosaurus and Tyrannosaurus had sharp teeth and strong jaws, which helped to make them the most powerful predators of the Age of Dinosaurs, which lasted from about 251 million to 65 million years ago.

Earth went through great changes during the Age of Dinosaurs. In the beginning, a vast supercontinent that scientists call Pangaea (*pan-JEE-uh*) was surrounded by a great ocean. Pangaea broke apart over millions of years, and the continents began to drift toward the positions they occupy today. There also were great changes among plants and animals. Early in the Age of Dinosaurs—some 251 million years ago—such seed plants as conifers, cycads, and ginkgoes were common. The first true mammals appeared, and crocodilians, frogs, insects, and lizards prospered. Flying reptiles called pterosaurs (*TEHR-uh-sawrz*) filled the skies. Plesiosaurs (*PLEE-see-uh-sawrz*) and other marine reptiles ruled the oceans. Later, flowering plants appeared and began to replace other seed plants in some areas, helping insects and mammals to thrive. Birds arose from small meat-eating dinosaurs and

## The Age of Dinosaurs

| Period | Triassic | Jurassic | Cretaceous |
|---|---|---|---|
| Began | 251 million years ago | 200 million years ago | 145 million years ago |
| Ended | 200 million years ago | 145 million years ago | 65 million years ago |
| Major Events | Dinosaurs first appeared but did not become common until the end of this period. | Dinosaurs became the largest animals everywhere on land, reaching their greatest size. | A mass extinction at the end of this period killed off all the dinosaurs except some birds. |

Dinosaurs first appeared during the Triassic Period. They became the largest, most successful land animals early in the Jurassic Period. The dinosaurs died out at the end of the Cretaceous Period. Together, these three periods make up the Mesozoic Era, the Age of Dinosaurs.

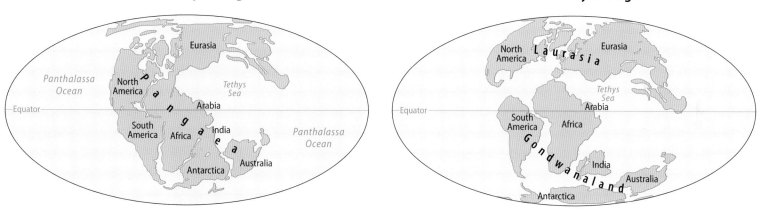

**200 million years ago**

Eurasia

Panthalassa Ocean

North America

Pangaea

Tethys Sea

Equator

Arabia

South America

Africa

India

Panthalassa Ocean

Antarctica

Australia

**100 million years ago**

North America

Laurasia

Eurasia

Equator

Tethys Sea

Arabia

South America

Africa

Gondwanaland

India

Australia

Antarctica

About 200 million years ago *(above left)* a supercontinent called Pangaea was surrounded by a vast ocean. Pangaea broke up into separate continents during the Age of Dinosaurs. By 100 million years ago *(above right),* the continents had begun to drift toward the positions they occupy today.

soon spread around the world. The first snakes appeared, along with modern bony fish.

Some dinosaurs flourished as conditions on Earth changed, while others struggled to adapt. Allosaurus and many other large theropods went extinct, but many theropods continued to thrive. Near the end of the Cretaceous Period, such large theropods as Tyrannosaurus still ruled the land. However, all these large fierce dinosaurs died out with the other dinosaurs, about 65 million years ago. Birds were the only descendants of dinosaurs to survive. Fortunately, we can learn about the world of fierce theropods through the fossils they left behind.

# Triassic Theropods

The earliest-known theropods appeared about 230 million years ago, in what is now South America, in the middle of the Triassic Period. In fact, the very first dinosaurs may have been theropods.

Triassic theropods were generally smaller and lighter than later theropods. Early theropods were slender, with flexible bodies and tails. They also generally had weaker claws, teeth, and jaws than many later theropods.

Triassic theropods were active, quick runners. They had to compete with many other kinds of animals for food and other resources. Many of these early theropods probably ate such food as eggs, insects, lizards, and small mammals. Early theropods had five fingers on their hands, though for many of them, the fourth and fifth fingers were probably too short to be of much use. Later theropods had fewer fingers—usually three—on their hands. Fewer fingers apparently worked just as well for grasping and raking prey.

Triassic theropods initially faced strong competition from reptiles and other animals. By the end of the Triassic Period, theropods had become the largest meat-eating animals on land.

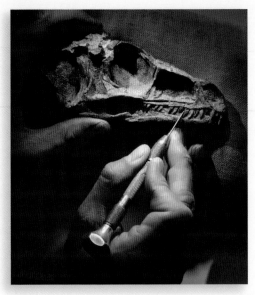

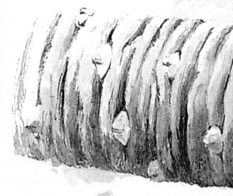

**A scientist delicately cleans the skull of Eoraptor *(left)*, one of the earliest-known dinosaurs. Eoraptor was a light, swift dinosaur that could chase down small prey *(opposite)*.**

**Eoraptor** *(EE-oh-RAP-tor)* is one of the oldest-known dinosaurs. It lived about 230 million years ago, in what is now Argentina. Eoraptor was roughly as big as a medium-sized dog. It had a slender body that reached about 3 feet (0.9 meter) in length. It probably weighed about 20 pounds (9 kilograms). All the later meat-eating dinosaurs arose from creatures much like Eoraptor.

FACT○SAUR

The name Eoraptor means "dawn thief." It first appeared at the dawn of the Age of Dinosaurs. It probably raided nests to steal eggs whenever it could.

Like other predators, Eoraptor had knifelike teeth in its jaws. However, the teeth at the front of its mouth were more leaf-shaped, almost like those of plant-eating dinosaurs.

Eoraptor dashed around on its long hind legs and used its grasping hands to catch lizards and other small animals. It may also have eaten plants.

Eoraptor had five fingers on its hands, though two of them were quite short. Most later theropods had only three fingers on each hand.

www.worldbook.com/dino6

## Herrerasaurus

*(huh-RARE-ah-SAWR-us)*
Herrerasaurus was one of the earliest dinosaurs, appearing about 230 million years ago.

## Staurikosaurus

*(STORE-ee-koh-SAWR-us)*
Staurikosaurus was a smaller theropod. It was probably a very fast predator that could chase down lizards and other small animals.

## Coelophysis

(SEE-low-FIE-sis)
Coleophysis was a graceful, fast-moving predator, with large eyes to help it find prey. It may have lived and hunted in packs.

## Saltopus

(SALT-oh-pus)
Saltopus was a small predator that ran on two legs. It had a long head, sharp teeth, and five clawed fingers. Scientists are not certain that Saltopus was a dinosaur—it may have been a closely related reptile instead.

Liliensternus had a unusual ridge running along the top of its snout. Although Liliensternus was large for its time, it had a slender body compared with other theropods.

# Liliensternus (LIL-ee-in-STER-nus)

was one of the largest predators of its time. It probably grew to about 17 feet (5.2 meters) long. It weighed up to about 300 pounds (130 kilograms).

Liliensternus had five fingers on its hands. Each finger ended in a sharp claw. These claws were probably used for both hunting and defense.

## FACT ○ SAUR

Liliensternus was named after a German doctor, H. R. von Lilienstern. He made many important fossil discoveries from the 1920's to the 1940's.

Liliensternus ran on its hind legs, and it probably could reach high speeds. It likely ate a variety of small animals, including some plant-eating dinosaurs.

13

Jurassic theropods such as Yangchuanosaurus *(left)* rank among the largest predators that have ever lived on land. A fossilized skeleton of Allosaurus *(opposite)* shows the fearsome claws and teeth of this large theropod.

# Jurassic Theropods

Theropods became the largest meat-eaters ever to live on land during the Jurassic Period, which lasted from about 200 million to 145 million years ago. Theropods spread throughout the world, becoming the most common predators.

Jurassic theropods were larger and more fearsome than their Triassic ancestors. Their jaws had become stronger, giving them a more powerful bite. Their legs were also more muscular. These features enabled many Jurassic theropods to hunt the enormous plant-eating dinosaurs that became widespread during the Jurassic Period. In addition, some of the Jurassic theropods may have lived and hunted in packs, much like wolves. Many likely hunted during the day, but there is evidence that some theropods hunted at night.

Early in the Jurassic Period, a group of small theropods gave rise to the first birds. In fact, scientists think that many theropods may have had simple feathers. These feathers were generally not used for flight. Instead, scientists believe the feathers provided warmth or were used for display, possibly to attract mates. Theropods also may have been warm-blooded, like modern birds.

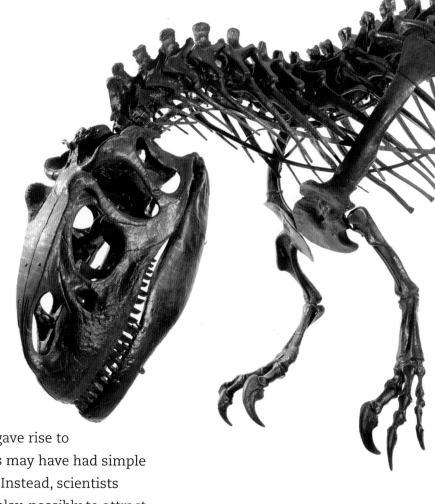

## Proceratosaurus

*(pro-ser-RAT-uh-SAWR-us)*
Proceratosaurus was a medium-sized theropod. It had a small crest on its nose, and its teeth curved strongly backward.

# FUN FACT

Cryolophosaurus is one of the few dinosaur fossils discovered in Antarctica—and the only meat-eating dinosaur found there.

## Cryolophosaurus

*krie-o-LOF-o-SAWR-us*
Cryolophosaurus had an unusual horizontal crest on its head. The crest ran from ear to ear. It was probably used for display, to attract mates.

## Megapnosaurus

*(meh-gap-no-SORE-us)*
Megapnosaurus was closely related to Coelophysis, and like Coelophysis, it also may have hunted and lived in packs. The size and structure of its eyes suggest that it may have been active mainly at night.

# Dilophosaurus (*die-loh-foh-SORE-us*)

was one of the larger early Jurassic theropods, reaching about 20 feet (6 meters) long. It has often been depicted in movies and video games, but it is often portrayed innaccurately.

Two long, thin crests grew on top of the head. These may have been used for display, possibly to attract mates.

Dilophosaurus was relatively slender and probably weighed 600 to 1,000 pounds (270 to 450 kilograms).

Dilophosaurus had long, sharp teeth, but its jaw was relatively weak. Its claws were its most useful weapons. Some scientists think Dilophosaurus fed on animal remains, rather than on prey it caught.

17

# Eustreptospondylus

*(you-STREP-toh-SPON-dy-lus)* was a medium-to-large theropod that lived from about 165 million to 160 million years ago. It probably had a typical theropod body, with small forelimbs, strong legs, and an upright posture.

Eustreptospondylus means "well-curved vertebrae." The name refers to the unusual shape of the dinosaur's backbones.

## FACT○SAUR

This dinosaur lived on small islands in the eastern Atlantic Ocean, near what is now the United Kingdom. Scientists think it hunted along the shore.

Eustreptospondylus is known from only one incomplete fossil. Scientists think the dinosaur was likely about 16 to 20 feet (5 to 6 meters) long. However, the bones may have been that of a juvenile, meaning adults would have grown larger.

Megalosaurus was the first dinosaur to be named, in 1824. Previously, people thought its bones belonged to a giant person!

## Megalosaurus

(MEG-*ah-lo-SAWR-us*)

Megalosaurus was a large theropod. It probably grew to about 30 feet (9 meters) long and weighed 2 tons (1.8 metric tons). It lived in the forests of what is now South America, during the middle of the Jurassic Period.

## Piatnitzkysaurus

(*pit-NYIT-skee-SAWR-us*)

Piatnitzkysaurus was closely related to Megalosaurus, and it lived around the same time. But Piatnitzkysaurus only reached about half the size of Megalosaurus. Also, it lived in forests in what is now western Europe.

## Afrovenator

*(AF-roh-vee-NAY-tor)*

Afrovenator was a large theropod that lived in what is now Africa. Scientists once thought it appeared during the Cretaceous Period. Many scientists now believe it appeared earlier, during the Jurassic Period.

**FUN FACT**

Employees of an oil company discovered the only known fossils of Gasosaurus. The dinosaur was named for the company's chief product, gasoline.

## Gasosaurus

*(GAS-oh-SAWR-us)*

Little is known about Gasosaurus because few of its fossils have been discovered. It was probably a medium-sized theropod. Some scientists think it might actually belong to the same dinosaur group as either Kaijangosaurus or Megalosaurus.

Ceratosaurus had a large bladelike horn on its nose. The horn was probably used for display rather than as a weapon.

# Ceratosaurus (ser-RAT-uh-SAWR-us)

was a medium-to-large theropod that lived toward the end of the Jurassic Period. It probably grew to between about 16 and 26 feet (5 to 8 meters). It had a series of bony plates on its back that probably served as armor.

Ceratosaurus had a long, flexible tail. This tail would have given Ceratosaurus improved ability to maneuver in the water. Scientists think it hunted for prey in streams, rivers, or lakes.

The main weapons of Ceratosaurus were its sharp teeth and its dangerous claws.

## FACT○SAUR

The name Ceratosaurus means "horned lizard," which refers to the large horn on the dinosaur's nose.

# Allosaurus *(al-oh-SAWR-us)* has

become one of the most famous of the meat-eating dinosaurs. It was a huge predator, in some cases reaching more than 30 feet (9 meters) long and weighing more than 2 tons (1.8 metric tons).

**FACT○SAUR**

The largest claws on Allosaurus were 10 inches (25 centimeters) in length.

The massive tail of Allosaurus helped the dinosaur keep its balance. Without its tail, Allosaurus would have fallen flat on its face.

Scientists believe Allosaurus had a relatively weak bite for an animal of its size. Evidence suggests that its bite was only as strong as that of a leopard, a much smaller animal.

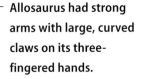

Allosaurus had strong arms with large, curved claws on its three-fingered hands.

www.worldbook.com/dino7

## Szechuanosaurus

*(sesh-WAHN-uh-SAWR-us)*
Szechuanosaurus is known only from four teeth, which were discovered in the Szechuan area of southwestern China. Many scientists think the teeth are actually from other kinds of dinosaur and that Szechuanosaurus was not a unique kind of dinosaur.

## Metriacanthosaurus

*(MET-ri-ah-CAN-thuh-SAWR-us)*
Metriacanthosaurus had a line of thin bones called spines sticking up from its backbone. These spines may have supported a hump or sail-like growth.

## Yangchuanosaurus

*(YANG-choo-WAN-oh-SAWR-us)*
Yangchuanosaurus was a fearsome predator that could grow to more than 30 feet (9 meters) long and weigh more than 2 tons (1.8 metric tons). It had a small crest that ran from the tip of its snout to its eyes.

DINO BITE

## Why Has Our Understanding of Dinosaurs Changed?

Not long ago, scientists who wrote about dinosaurs described them as sluggish, unintelligent lizards. For years, dinosaurs were thought to have been clumsy animals that dragged their tails on the ground.

Today, we believe dinosaurs were quick and graceful. Many dinosaurs were intelligent animals that lived in groups and provided care for their young. Why has our understanding of dinosaurs changed?

For most of human history, no one knew that dinosaurs ever existed. People who found dinosaur bones may have thought they belonged to such mythical creatures as dragons, griffins, and other terrible monsters.

In the early 1800's, scientists began to study dinosaur fossils. They recognized similarities between dinosaur bones and the bones of living reptiles. In 1841, English scientist Sir Richard Owen suggested that the fossils came from a group of prehistoric reptiles unlike any living animals. He called these creatures the Dinosauria, which means "terribly great lizards."

Most early *paleontologists* (scientists who study prehistoric life) assumed that dinosaurs were like lizards in other ways. For example, they thought dinosaurs were cold-blooded and slow-moving. They believed that plant-eating sauropods were too large to support their weight on land, so these giants must have spent most of their time in swamps. Similarly, many early paleontologists thought Tyrannosaurus was too slow and clumsy to hunt.

Instead, they thought Tyrannosaurus was a scavenger that fed on the remains of dead dinosaurs, basking in the sun between meals like a giant lizard.

Many early paleontologists believed that dinosaurs became extinct because they could not compete with mammals. Some viewed dinosaurs as primitive animals that were doomed to die out.

Today, paleontologists know from fossil evidence that sauropods did not live in swamps or drag their tails. Most sauropods preferred dry land. They had legs shaped like columns, and they walked erect like an elephant, with the head and tail well above the ground. Some moved about in herds. Also, most paleontologists now believe that Tyrannosaurus was an active predator that walked with its head forward and its tail straight back.

Scientists now know that dinosaurs did not became extinct because they were primitive. Many now believe that dinosaurs died out after a large asteroid struck Earth.

Paleontologists have also learned that certain dinosaurs evolved into birds. Many of the features we associate with birds first appeared among the theropods, including feathers. Many theropods had feathers of some kind— perhaps even Tyrannosaurus. Like birds, theropods may have been warm-blooded and quite active. Many dinosaurs also made nests and cared for their young. Today, most paleontologists believe many dinosaurs were more like giant predatory chickens than overgrown lizards.

This 1939 painting by famed artist Charles R. Knight shows sauropods dragging their tails and living submerged in a swamp. Scientists no longer believe this depiction of sauropods is accurate.

# Cretaceous Theropods

Theropods flourished during the Cretaceous Period, which lasted from about 145 million to 65 million years ago. In fact, we know of more theropods from the late Cretaceous Period than from any other time during the Age of Dinosaurs.

As the continents drifted apart, the widening oceans created barriers that few animals could cross. Because of this geographic separation, many new kinds of dinosaurs appeared, with different ways of life. Some were long-limbed and had toothless beaks to feed on eggs and insects. Some had large claws on their hands and ate fish. Others lived in deserts and probably hunted small mammals and reptiles. The largest theropods were fearsome predators that could attack even the biggest of the giant, plant-eating dinosaurs called sauropods.

The large theropods reached their peak with the fearsome tyrannosaurs (tih-RAN-uh-SAWRS), a name which means "tyrant lizard." Tyrannosaurs were highly intelligent, with sharp vision and a keen sense of smell. Their jaws were so strong that they could crush bone. The tyrannosaurs lived in what is now Asia and North America. At the same time, other large meat-eating theropods thrived in what are now South America and Africa. These theropods were the top predators in their lands, just as tyrannosaurs ruled their continents.

The fossilized skull of Tyrannosaurus *(below)* shows its fearsome teeth, which reached the size of bananas. Chilantaisaurus *(opposite)* was another large, dangerous theropod of the Cretaceous Period.

## Baryonyx

*(BAYR-ee-ON-iks)*
Baryonyx was a large theropod with a skull and snout that resembled those of a crocodile. It probably used its strong, hooked claws to spear fish.

## Becklespinax

*(BECK-el-SPY-nax)*
Becklespinax is known from only a handful of incomplete fossils. Scientists think it was a large theropod. It may have had a spiny sail along its back.

## Suchomimus

*(SOOK-o-MIME-us)*
Suchomimus had a crocodile-shaped head, with large claws, and a sail-shaped growth on its back. It resembled Baryonyx, and some scientists think they may actually represent the same group of dinosaurs.

Acrocanthosaurus had a tall sail-shaped growth running down the length of its back. This sail may have helped to control body temperature. It also may have been used for display.

# Acrocanthosaurus

(*AK-roh-CAN-thuh-SAWR-us*) was an enormous meat-eating dinosaur that could grow to 40 feet (12 meters) long. It weighed from 3 to 7 tons (3 to 6 metric tons).

The colossal head of Acrocanthosaurus was full of daggerlike teeth. The head was more than 4 feet (1.25 meters) long.

Like many other large theropods, Acrocanthosaurus probably had a good sense of smell, which it relied on to find prey.

**FACT○SAUR**

Acrocanthosaurus was the top predator of its time. Scientists have found many footprints in North America that were probably made by this dinosaur.

# Spinosaurus (SPINE-oh-SAWR-us) was a

gigantic predator that lived in what is now northern Africa. It was probably the largest of the theropods. Some scientists estimate that it reached up to about 60 feet (18 meters) long. It probably weighed about 6 to 9 tons (5 to 8 metric tons).

Scientists are not sure why Spinosaurus had a large sail-like growth on its back. It may have helped the dinosaur to control its body temperature. The sail may also have been used for display.

Spinosaurus may have hunted both on land and in the water. The structure of its skull, including its raised nostrils, would have helped it to hunt well in water.

Spinosaurus had a long, narrow snout, like that of a crocodile. Its many sharp teeth were relatively small.

FACT◯SAUR

The first known Spinosaurus fossils were kept in a German museum. They were destroyed by bombs during World War II (1939-1945).

www.worldbook.com/dino8

## Carcharodontosaurus

*(kahr-KAR-o-DONT-o-SAWR-us)*

Carcharodontosaurus was one of the largest theropods. It grew to more than 40 feet (12 meters) long, and it likely weighed from 6 to 8 tons (5 to 7 metric tons). It lived in what are now Africa and South America.

## Chilantaisaurus

*(chee-LAWN-ti-SAWR-us)*

Chilantaisaurus was a large theropod that lived in modern-day Asia. It had large, hooked claws on its forelimbs. Scientists have only poor-quality fossils of this dinosaur, so many questions remain about how it lived and appeared.

## Giganotosaurus

*(jie-GAN-oh-toe-SAWR-us)*

Giganotosaurus was closely related to Carchardontosaurus and had a similar build. However, it lived in what is now North Africa, and it was not quite as large.

# Abelisaurus

*(ah-BEL-i-SAWR-us)*
Abelisaurus is known from only a single, partial skull found in South America. Scientists think it was a relatively large theropod, probably reaching 25 to 30 feet (7.5 to 9 meters) long.

## FUN FACT

The name Alectrosaurus means "unmarried lizard." At the time it was discovered, Alectrosaurus was unlike any other predator found in Asia.

# Alectrosaurus

*(ah-LECK-troh-SAWR-us)*
Alectrosaurus was an early, Asian ancestor of the famous Tyrannosaurus. It was only half as tall, but Alectrosaurus was just as well armed, with large jaws, many teeth, and sharp claws.

The name Carnotaurus means "meat-eating bull." The dinosaur was named for the two stubby, bull-like horns on its head. These might have been used for display or in fights with rivals.

# Carnotaurus (KAR-no-TAWR-us)

was a large theropod that lived in modern-day Argentina, about 75 million to 70 million years ago. It grew to about 25 feet (7.5 meters) in length and weighed between 1 and 2 tons (0.9 and 1.8 metric tons).

## FACT◯SAUR

Carnotaurus had a massive head, but its jaws were slender and its teeth rather weak. Some scientists think it might have scavenged animal remains.

Carnotaurus had long, relatively slender legs, with powerful thighs. Scientists think its tail was particularly strong and straight. This combination of features might have allowed it to reach running speeds as fast as 30 miles (48 kilometers) per hour!

Carnotaurus had unusually short arms, even for a theropod. Each arm ended in four fingers. The fingers had no claws and could not move.

www.worldbook.com/dino9

**Dryptosaurus** (DRIP-*toe*-SAWR-*us*) was a large theropod that lived toward the end of the Cretaceous Period. It probably grew to about 20 to 25 feet (6 to 7.5 meters) in length and weighed from about 1 and 1.5 tons (0.9 to 1.4 metric tons).

The large skull of Dryptosaurus was filled with hollow spaces to reduce its weight.

## FACT ◯ SAUR

Dryptosaurus was the first theropod discovered in North America. Only partial remains of a single skeleton have been found.

Dryptosaurus had relatively long arms for a theropod. Each arm had three fingers, which ended in 8-inch (20-centimeter) claws. Its name, which means "tearing lizard," refers to these fearsome claws.

34

## Deinocheirus

*(DINE-oh-KIE-rus)*
Deinocheirus was a large theropod with arms that grew 8 feet (2.4 meters) long. The arms ended in strongly curved claws.

## Albertosaurus

*(al-BUR-toe-SAWR-us)*
Albertosaurus was a large theropod that lived in modern-day Canada. It was related to Tyrannosaurus. However, Albertosaurus was not as large or as heavy as Tyrannosaurus.

### FUN FACT

Scientists have found only the arms and a few other bones of Deinocheirus. As a result, they can only guess how the rest of its body looked.

## Aublysodon

*(aw-BLIS-oh-don)*
Scientists have found only the fossilized teeth of Aublysodon. They once thought the teeth belonged to a unique theropod closely related to Tyrannosaurus. However, many scientists now suspect the teeth may belong to another theropod.

## Alioramus

(AL-ee-uh-RAY-mus)
Alioramus was another close relative of Tyrannosaurus. However, it was much smaller than other tyrannosaurs, and it had a much weaker bite.

## Tarbosaurus

(TAR-bow-SAWR-us)
Tarbosaurus was a massive theropod and an Asian cousin of Tyrannosaurus. However, some scientists now argue that Tarbosaurus fossils really belong to Tyrannosaurus.

## Nanotyrannus

(NAN-oh-tie-RAN-us)
Fossils of Nanotyrannus may simply be those of a young Tyrannosaurus. Nanotyrannus had a large jaw full of serrated teeth and short arms with sharp claws.

The name Tyrannosaurus means "tyrant lizard." It had one of the most powerful bites of any known land animal. Its jaws could crush bone.

# Tyrannosaurus

(*tie-RAN-oh-SAWR-us*) was one of the most fearsome of all dinosaur predators. It grew to about 40 feet (12 meters) in length and about 12 feet (3.7 meters) at the hips. It weighed about 7 tons (6.3 metric tons). Tyrannosaurus lived in what is now North America.

Tyrannosaurus held its long tail out to counterbalance its heavy body.

Tyrannosaurus was likely an active hunter that could run a short distance. It may have waited in ambush, to lunge at prey with its powerful jaws and the sharp claws on its two-fingered hands.

Tyrannosaurus had keen vision, a good sense of smell, and a larger brain than other theropods of similar size. The head was nearly 5 feet (1.5 meters) long, and the teeth were as large as bananas.

www.worldbook.com/dino10

## What Is a Fossil?

The Age of Dinosaurs ended about 65 million years ago, long before there were human beings on Earth. Yet *paleontologists* (scientists who study prehistoric life) are able to describe how dinosaurs looked and moved. They can tell us about prehistoric forests and strange plants. In museums, we can see the skeletons of dinosaurs that died many millions of years ago. Why haven't their bones turned to dust?

The bones have survived as fossils. Fossils are the remains or the marks of living things that died long ago. Paleontologists have made remarkable discoveries about dinosaurs and the history of life by studying fossils.

The vast majority of plants and animals die and decay without leaving any trace. Microbes break down soft tissues such as leaves or flesh, and so these tissues rarely form fossils. Even most hard parts, such as bones, teeth, shells, or wood, are eventually worn away. But when plant or animal remains are quickly buried, they may be preserved from decay. These remains may become fossilized.

Most dinosaur fossils form as part of *sedimentary* (layered) rock. This process begins when dinosaur remains are buried in sediments—that is, the mud or sand that settles out of water. After the remains are buried, water may seep down through the sediments and deposit minerals in the bones.

**Paleontologist Luis Chiappe works to recover the fossilized skull of a Protoceratops dinosaur in Mongolia.**

Over thousands of years, more and more sediment layers are deposited on the layer containing the fossil. The weight of the upper layers presses down on the fossil-bearing sediment and eventually turns it into rock. Later, erosion may expose layers of sedimentary rock, revealing the fossilized dinosaur bones for paleontologists to find.

During the late 1800's and early 1900's, many dinosaur fossils were discovered in western North America, Europe, Asia, and Africa. Today, many new dinosaur discoveries are being made in China, Canada, Mongolia, Argentina, and parts of Africa. These fossil discoveries have greatly increased the number of known dinosaurs. Scientists discover and describe the fossils of several new kinds of dinosaur every year.

Dinosaur fossils usually consist only of bones or other hard parts, such as teeth or armored plates known as scutes. Rarely, dinosaurs are fossilized with softer parts preserved. In 1999, paleontologists working in North Dakota discovered the remains of a hadrosaur they named Edmontosaurus that was mummified before fossilization began. Millions of years ago, the dinosaur died on the banks of a sandy riverbed and its body was quickly buried. Waterlogged sediment entombed the body before it could decay. The fossilized remains were so well preserved that scientists have been able to examine its skin, muscles, ligaments, tendons, and even its internal organs. Other mummified fossils have preserved the remains of the stomach, giving us a glimpse of the dinosaurs' final meals.

# Where to Find Dinosaurs

The Natural History Museum of Los Angeles County, Los Angeles, California

## Museums in the United States

### ARIZONA

**The Arizona Museum of Natural History**
http://azmnh.org/Exhibits/dinohall
53 N. Macdonald
Mesa, Arizona 85201

Theropods, sauropods, and other dinosaurs rule at Dinosaur Hall. Visitors can also explore prehistoric Arizona in the Walk Through Time exhibit.

### CALIFORNIA

**Natural History Museum of Los Angeles County**
http://www.nhm.org/site/explore-exhibits
900 Exposition Boulevard.
Los Angeles, California 90007

After you explore the fossils and skeletons in Dinosaur Hall, get a behind-the-scenes look at how the exhibits are made in the Dino Lab.

**University of California Museum of Paleontology**
http://www.ucmp.berkeley.edu
1101 Valley Life Sciences Building
Berkeley, California 94720

Many of this museum's exhibits are viewable online as well as in person.

### COLORADO

**The Denver Museum of Nature & Science**
http://www.dmns.org
2001 Colorado Boulevard
Denver, Colorado 80205

Dynamic re-creations of ancient environments as well as hands-on fossils tell the story of prehistoric life.

**Dinosaur National Monument**
http://www.nps.gov/dino
4545 Hwy 40, Dinosaur National Monument
Dinosaur, Colorado 81610

The Dinosaur National Monument is located in both Colorado and Utah. Its world-famous Carnegie Dinosaur Quarry, home to nearly 1,500 dinosaur fossils, is on the Utah side.

### CONNECTICUT

**Dinosaur State Park**
http://www.dinosaurstatepark.org
400 West Street
Rocky Hill, Connecticut 06067

Here you will find one of the largest dinosaur track sites in North America. Visitors can also explore the Arboretum, which contains more than 250 species of plants—many dating back to prehistoric eras.

**The Yale Peabody Museum of Natural History**
http://peabody.yale.edu
170 Whitney Avenue
New Haven, Connecticut 06511-8902

Don't miss the Great Hall of Dinosaurs with its famous "Age of Reptiles" mural—one of the largest in the world.

## GEORGIA

### The Fernbank Museum of Natural History
http://www.fernbankmuseum.org
767 Clifton Road NE
Atlanta, Georgia 30307

See a Giganotosaurus and other dinosaurs in the Giants of the Mesozoic exhibit.

## ILLINOIS

### The Chicago Children's Museum at Navy Pier
http://www.chicagochildrensmuseum.org
700 East Grand Avenue
Chicago, Illinois 60611

Kids of all ages can explore a re-creation of an actual dinosaur excavation, including searching for bones in an excavation pit.

### The Discovery Center Museum
http://www.discoverycentermuseum.org
711 North Main Street
Rockford, Illinois 61103

Visitors will enjoy the simulated dinosaur dig at this children's museum.

### The Field Museum
http://fieldmuseum.org
1400 S Lake Shore Drive
Chicago, Illinois 60605

Chicago's Field Museum is home to Sue, the largest and most complete Tyrannosaurus rex skeleton ever discovered.

The Field Museum,
Chicago, Illinois

## INDIANA

### The Dinosphere at the Children's Museum of Indianapolis
http://www.childrensmuseum.org/themuseum/dinosphere
3000 North Meridian Street
Indianapolis, Indiana 46208

Experience the world of the dinosaurs with family digs, fossil preparation, and sensory exhibits.

## MAINE

### The Maine Discovery Museum
http://www.mainediscoverymuseum.org
74 Main Street
Bangor, Maine 04401

Young visitors to this children's museum can explore the world of paleontology at the museum's new Dino Dig exhibit.

## MASSACHUSETTS

### The Museum of Science, Boston
http://www.mos.org
1 Science Park
Boston, Massachusetts 02114

A 23-foot- (7-meter-) long Triceratops specimen, found in the Dakota Badlands, is just one of the fascinating fossils on display here.

## MICHIGAN

### The University of Michigan Museum of Natural History
http://www.lsa.umich.edu/ummnh
1109 Geddes Avenue
Ann Arbor, Michigan 48109

Michigan's largest collection of prehistoric specimens lives in the Museum of Natural History's rotunda and galleries.

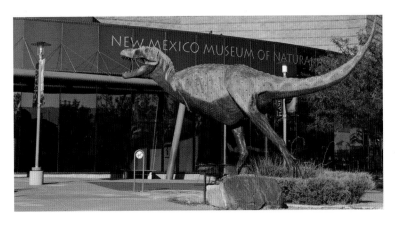

The New Mexico Museum of Natural History, Albuquerque, New Mexico

### The Academy of Natural Sciences of Drexel University

http://www.ansp.org/visit/exhibits/dinosaur-hall

1900 Benjamin Franklin Parkway

Philadelphia, Pennsylvania 19103

Impressive skeletons of massive dinosaurs stalk Drexel's Dinosaur Hall. Visitors can also visit the fossil lab to learn how fossils are prepared and studied.

### The Carnegie Museum of Natural History

http://www.carnegiemnh.org/exhibitions/dinosaurs.html

4400 Forbes Avenue

Pittsburgh, Pennsylvania 15213

The Dinosaurs in the Their Time exhibit features scientifically accurate re-creations of environments from the Age of Dinosaurs, organized chronologically.

### SOUTH DAKOTA

### The Children's Museum of South Dakota

http://www.prairieplay.org

521 4th Street

Brookings, South Dakota 57006

Meet Mama and Max, a pair of full-sized animatronic T. rex dinosaurs, and try your hand at a dinosaur dig.

### MINNESOTA

### The Science Museum of Minnesota

http://www.smm.org

120 W. Kellogg Boulevard

St. Paul, Minnesota 55102

Do some hands-on fossil exploration at the Paleontology Lab, then get inside the jaws of a giant T. rex to simulate its mighty bite!

### NEW MEXICO

### The New Mexico Museum of Natural History and Science

http://www.nmnaturalhistory.org

1801 Mountain Road NW

Albuquerque, New Mexico 87104

The Timetracks exhibit covers the Triassic, Jurassic, and Cretaceous periods as part of a journey from the origins of life on Earth to the present day.

### NEW YORK

### The American Museum of Natural History

http://www.amnh.org

Central Park West at 79th Street

New York, New York 10024

This museum's famous Fossil and Dinosaur halls house nearly 1 million specimens.

### NORTH CAROLINA

### North Carolina Museum of Natural Sciences

http://naturalsciences.org

11 West Jones Street

Raleigh, North Carolina 27601

Home to Willo the Thescalosaurus, an Acrocanthosaurus, and four fossilized whales.

**The Creative Discovery Museum**
http://www.cdmfun.org
321 Chestnut Street
Chattanooga, Tennessee 37402

The Creative Discovery Museum's Excavation Station lets young visitors dig their own dinosaur bones.

**The Houston Museum of Natural Science**
http://www.hmns.org
5555 Hermann Park Drive
Houston, Texas 77030

A world-class Hall of Paleontology includes more than 30 new dinosaurs and many other prehistoric creatures in "action" poses.

**The Natural History Museum of Utah**
http://nhmu.utah.edu
301 Wakara Way
Salt Lake City, Utah 84108

The paleontology collections at Utah's Natural History Museum include more than 30,000 specimens.

**The Virginia Museum of Natural History**
http://www.vmnh.net
21 Starling Avenue
Martinsville, Virginia 24112

Detailed models and interactive features accompany the dinosaur exhibits.

**The National Museum of Natural History—Smithsonian Institution**
http://www.mnh.si.edu
10th Street & Constitution Avenue NW
Washington, D.C. 20560

Visit the Hall of Paleontology—free of charge—to come face-to-face with dinosaurs, fossil mammals, and fossil plants.

**The Wyoming Dinosaur Center**
http://www.wyodino.org
110 Carter Ranch Road
Thermopolis, Wyoming 82443

The combined museum and dig site offers daylong digs for visitors of all ages.

The Carnegie Museum of Natural History, Pittsburgh, Pennsylvania

# Museums in Canada

## ALBERTA

### The Royal Tyrrell Museum
http://www.tyrrellmuseum.com
1500 North Dinosaur Trail
Drumheller, Alberta T0J 0Y0, Canada

Tyrannosaurus rex, Triceratops, Quetzalcoatlus (a pterodactyloid), and many other fossils can be found here.

## ONTARIO

### The Canadian Museum of Nature
http://nature.ca/en/home
240 McLeod Street
Ottawa, Ontario, Canada

Explore the lives—and the eventual extinction—of the dinosaurs in the Fossil Gallery.

### The London Children's Museum
http://www.londonchildrensmuseum.ca
21 Wharncliffe Road South
London, Ontario N6J 4G5, Canada

The Dinosaur Gallery includes demonstrations, fossil casts, and replicas of many dinosaurs from the Jurassic Period.

### The Royal Ontario Museum
http://www.rom.on.ca
100 Queen's Park
Toronto, Ontario, M5S 2C6, Canada

These exhibits feature dinosaurs and other fossils from the Jurassic and Cretaceous periods.

## QUEBEC

### The Redpath Museum
http://www.mcgill.ca/redpath
859 Sherbrooke Street West
Montreal, Quebec, Canada

Learn about the animals that roamed prehistoric Quebec as well as about many types of dinosaur.

# Museums in the United Kingdom

### Dinosaurland Fossil Museum
http://www.dinosaurland.co.uk/
Coombe Street, Lyme Regis
Dorset, DT7 3PY, United Kingdom

Dinosaurland includes a large collection of Jurassic fossils and dinosaur models.

### The Dinosaur Museum
http://www.thedinosaurmuseum.com/
Icen Way, Dorchester
Dorset, DT1 1EW, United Kingdom

Highlights include kid-friendly, hands-on computer displays, dinosaur skeletons, and a wide range of fossils.

### The National Museum of Scotland
http://www.nms.ac.uk/
Chambers Street
Edinburgh, EH1 1JF, United Kingdom

Allosaurus and Triceratops skeletons are part of a prehistory exhibit, along with dinosaur footprints and a "dino dig" for young visitors.

### The Natural History Museum
http://www.nhm.ac.uk/
Cromwell Road, London SW7 5BD

The elaborate dinosaur gallery includes four animatronic dinosaurs.

### Oxford University Museum of Natural History
http://www.oum.ox.ac.uk/
Parks Road, Oxford,
OX1 3PW, United Kingdom

The outstanding collection of dinosaur fossils and skeletons includes a Camptosaurus, Cetiosaurus, Eustreptospondylus, Iguanodon, Lexovisaurus, Megalosaurus, and a Metriacanthosaurus.

## Museums in Australia

### The Australian Museum

http://australianmuseum.net.au
6 College Street Sydney
New South Wales 2010, Australia

A permanent dinosaur exhibit features high-tech interactive displays, animatronic dinosaurs, and a paleontology lab that is open to young visitors.

### The Melbourne Museum

http://museumvictoria.com.au/
melbournemuseum
11 Nicholson St. Carlton
Victoria, 3053, Australia

A kid-friendly Dinosaur Walk exhibition brings the prehistoric world to life.

### The National Dinosaur Museum

http://www.nationaldinosaurmuseum.com.au
Gold Creek Road and Barton Highway
Nicholls, Australia Capital Terrority 2913

Home to the largest permanent display of dinosaur and other prehistoric fossil material in Australia.

### The South Australian Museum

http://www.samuseum.sa.gov.au
North Terrace

Adelaide, South Australia 5000, Australia
Walk through a paleontology collection that includes more than 40,000 specimens.

The Natural History
Museum, London
(Opposite)


The Canterbury Museum,
Christchurch, New
Zealand (left)

## Museums in New Zealand

### Canterbury Museum

http://www.canterburymuseum.com/
Christchurch Central, Christchurch 8013
New Zealand

The Geology gallery features fossils and an introduction to the fearsome marine reptiles of New Zealand's prehistory.

# Additional Resources

## Books

### Dinosaur Discovery: Everything You Need to Be a Paleontologist
by Christopher McGowan and Erica Lyn Schmidt (Simon and Schuster Books for Young Readers, 2011)

Activities and experiments show readers how paleontologists examine ancient fossils.

### Dinosaur Mountain: Digging into the Jurassic Age
by Deborah Kogan Ray (Frances Foster Books/Farrar, Straus, Giroux, 2010)

Follow fossil expert Earl Douglass on his 1908 hunt for dinosaur bones, which led to the discovery of several amazing skeletons.

### Dinosaurs
by John A. Long (Simon and Schuster Books for Young Readers, 2007)

3-D model imaging helps bring dinosaurs to life in this informative book.

### Dinosaurs: The Most Complete, Up-to-Date Encyclopedia for Dinosaur Lovers of All Ages
by Thomas R. Holtz and Luis V. Rey (Random House, 2007)

A reference guide to all things dinosaur, from fossil hunting to evolution.

### The Discovery and Mystery of a Dinosaur Named Jane
by Judith Williams (Enslow Publishers, 2008)

This book traces the journey of one dinosaur's skeleton, from discovery to museum.

## DVD's

### Bizarre Dinosaurs
(National Geographic, 2009)

Paleontologists lead you on a tour of some of the strangest dinosaurs to ever walk the Earth.

### Dinosaur Collection
(Discovery-Gaiam, 2011)

Computer-animated simulations paint a vivid picture of dinosaurs and their world.

### Dinosaurs Unearthed
(National Geographic, 2007)

Watch the examination of a mummified dinosaur for a new understanding of how dinosaurs looked, moved, and lived.

# Index

# Photo Credits

Illustrations by Amber Books
and WORLD BOOK (Ian Jackson, The Art Agency)